THIS IS FOR THE

MOSTLESS

THIS IS FOR THE

MOSTLESS

JASON MAGABO PEREZ

WordTech Editions

Published by WordTech Editions
P.O. BOX 541106
Cincinnati, OH 45254-1106

ISBN: 978-1-62549-243-2

Poetry Editor: Kevin Walzer
Business Editor: Lori Jareo

Cover Design: Amy Abito
Interior Design: Jason Magabo Perez
Author Illustration: Cal Tabuena-Frolli

www.wordtechweb.com

for my lovely & resilient parents, Yonie & Doro

Mostly are we mostless,
And neverness is all we become.

JOSÉ GARCIA VILLA

CONTENTS

Violent Hero

We share an apartment with hundreds of ipis,

ipis in the front room, ipis in the back,

ipis crawling on the kitchen counter,

ipis marching across the carpet,

ipis on the VCR, ipis inside

the VCR, ipis on the plastic plants,

ipis up & down the Venetian blinds,

ipis in the garbage disposal, ipis, ipis,

ipis on the bags of rice, so many ipis huddled

in the mouth of an empty vinegar bottle.

Let's say it's 1990. Redlands, California.

I'm nine years old.

I'm in the master bedroom.

It smells of Raid & bleach & fried fish.

My brother has just copped the hottest, most groundbreaking single to ever hit Kmart! The West Coast Rap All-Stars—Tone-Loc, Michel'le, Ice-T, JJ Fad, Young MC, MC Hammer, NWA, Too $hort, etc.—have united under one powerful thesis:

"We're all in the same gang."

Same.

Gang.

Say what?

This single drops at a time when I'm scared to rock the wrong colors, like the wrong red on my red Bulls jacket, like the wrong blue of my Jordache jeans, like the wrong combination of black & gray.

This drops at a time when my fellow third graders are claiming the sets & hoods & barrios of their dead uncles.

A time when we're beginning to notice that we are so death & so penniless.

So penny-skinned.

Some of us feel ugly & stupid.

Some of us talk mad shit like we matter.

Some of us hide.

Once upon a time, in 1990, I'm hiding in the master bedroom & replaying this perfect song on my mama's alarm clock radio—this perfect song helps me hope:

End the violence.

We are all in the same gang.

I got mad hope that this song can save the world.

& what gets me most is the impeccable verse of Eazy-E.

I decide to record my own version.

I grab my brother's boombox & a blank Memorex tape.

I set the boombox on the bed.

I load the blank Memorex tape into the recording deck.

I press *record* & *pause*.

I press *rewind* on the alarm clock radio & find Eazy's verse. *Stop*.

I release *pause* on the boombox to start recording.

I press *play* on the alarm clock radio.

Respectfully, I begin to spit my lungs out:

"Last but not least, yo, Jason's no sellout…"

I recite bar for bar Eazy's high-pitched & nasally but G'd up & captivating flow.

In this brief narrative, Eazy, now I, address a hypothetical young gangster, a gangster who I might see rolling through our apartment complex, a gangster from whom I run, from whom I hide, for whom I cry, for whom I pray.

Emulating Eazy I narrate the life & sudden death of that hypothetical young gangster, whose mother is mourning & mourning—her son is dead now, nothing "but a zero / take notes from Jason P., the violent hero."

(I'm not actually the 'violent hero.' I'd cry myself to pieces if I ever had to be this confident in teaching my brother's dead homies some act right.)

I hit *stop* on both machines.

I *rewind* my new recording & cue it up.

I hurry to the kitchen & grab my mama.

I urge my mama to her room & press *play*.

What could my mama possibly be thinking?

Perhaps she is taken aback by my command of the English language. & my command of Compton Black vernacular no less.

Perhaps she is heartbroken that her bunso is in desperate need of such hope.

Perhaps she herself hopes to Jesus & Mary that she will never become the mother in the song, mourning the death of one of her babies.

What does my mama make of my creativity?

Of my desire to record my hope for a new world?

Am I a budding rapper? Am I a Filipino Bow Wow before Lil Bow Wow becomes Bow Wow? Or before Bow Wow emerges as Lil Adorable Ass Baby G Bow Wow on Arsenio Hall in 1993?

Regardless of my mama's hopes & fears, regardless of my becoming, my mama says, as she wipes & wipes dead ipis legs from the nightstand:

"Wow, anak. Ang ganda! You are so good in English."

Cough Drop: An Artifact

for Fortunata A. Perez (1916-2006)

This, I imagine, is how I've begun to associate the smell of eucalyptus with perpetual melancholia.

It is 1972.

I don't exist. Yet.

But Epifanio, who later when I'm born becomes my *late* grandfather, certainly does. Exist.

& most importantly, Epifanio is married to Fortunata, who later when I'm born becomes my grandmother.

I imagine Fortunata, not yet my grandmother, in 1972, at the airport in Manila, which at this point is not yet Ninoy Aquino International, to smell of stale cigarette smoke & beer, & to be wearing thick plastic eyeglass frames, her hair tied back tightly, her pantalones pressed neatly, her dark red lipstick perfect, & her hopes & fears of migration nestled in the crevices of her tiny little face.

Epifanio, I imagine, is not nervous at all.

Epifanio, I'll later hear, promises & promises to meet his beloved Fortunata in the States once their children—one of whom will become my father when I'm born, the rest of whom will become my aunties & uncles—are settled.

Today, in 1972, Fortunata is leaving under the condition that Epifanio, her beloved, will follow.

It is more than likely that Fortunata doesn't want to migrate to the States.

I'm too old, she is thinking. *It's not worth it.*

Fortunata has heard so very many things about others who have migrated.

The States, I'm sure she has heard, is a scary place.

Fortunata, I'm certain, has had nightmares of being robbed & pushed on the street by odd-looking people who have soft hair & angular noses. Those odd-looking people who have soft hair & angular noses are the same odd-looking people who have soft hair & angular noses, & the nerve, & the history, & U.S. Passports, & look so lost yet so entitled here, in 1972, at the airport in Manila.

So, here, at the airport in Manila, Fortunata hugs & hugs Epifanio with focus & intention.

"This," jokes Epifanio, "maybe will gonna be the last time you will gonna see me."

&…it is. The last time.

When Fortunata, who still isn't yet my grandmother, lands in Chicago, one of her sons, one of my later uncles, presents the news: "Tatay is sick."

Days later, it is revealed: "Tatay has had a heart attack."

Tatay, or Epifanio, who later becomes my *late* grandfather who I'll have never met, the love of Fortunata's life, sadly, has died.

Fortunata, in 1972, is looking down.

Fortunata is biting her lip.

Fortunata is reaching into her purse & grabbing a yellow Halls cough drop, eucalyptus-flavored.

Fortunata is now unwrapping the cough drop, is now placing it on her tongue & is now, in 1972, & I'm sure in her future grave which exists in this very now, cursing & cursing the States by biting, biting down so hard, with so much focus, so much vigor, & so much intention, that we, all of us, from then & from now, might never ever feel like we ever belonged *here*.

Crayoning the King: On Discipline

1.

I'm in kindergarten. McKinley Elementary School, Redlands, California. It's morning. It's hot. It's dry. We're in a classroom of hardened carpet & cold tile, a holding cell for crybabies who miss mommy. We've been learning how to follow rules, how to open miniature milk cartons without spilling, how to square dance like white people who wear funny-looking boots. I'm identified as bright, a rule-follower, perhaps one of the muddy-haired brown kids that the white teacher can save. Today, we're coloring the king. The king is plump with a beardly beard & a pointy nose. I crayon the king's skin a gentle orange & his beard a harsh copper. I bite the method of some of my classmates—first, I trace the inside of the king's outline, then I color within the line of my own tracing. Eventually, I color the king's cape red. This time, I lay the red crayon on its side & begin shading. A gorgeous texture emerges— a vastness of uneven strokes, punctures & embossments caused by pebbles & lint pressing against the underside of the paper. I finish & hurry to show my teacher. "I'm disappointed," she says. She runs her fingers across the now three-dimensional cape. "I expected better from you," she says. Never mind that my crayoning shows traces, the process of my art, the transparency of my method—a very process-not-product-anti-fetishist kind of performance, no? But my teacher remains disappointed. She tries to smooth out the cape against the edge of her desk. She expects me to color more cleanly, to hold the crayon properly, like a good pupil, like a good subject. I have failed her. Something. I cry.

2.

I'm in eighth grade & today we've been invited to wear our histories. Proudly. My mestizo homie says he's wearing cut-off jeans & slippers "like they do in the province." No offense, but this fool *passes* so he just looks like one of them anti-establishment white kids who choose to run away from their privilege & not comb their ratty hair & be homeless. Others claim that their history is right here, right now. So, they wear baggy sweatpants, their illegible tag names scribbled down each leg. I wear a T-shirt with a monkey-eating eagle on it. I bought it at the Filipino supermarket. I drape a folded Philippine flag over my shoulder. Toward the end of lunchtime, I lend my homie, Benny, who is Black & Filipino, my flag. Benny folds the flag as much as he can & hangs it from his back pocket. The principal snatches the flag from Benny. I cry. I try to get my flag back. The principal tells me that I let Benny display our history in such a disrespectful manner. But it's not like I was plunging my flag into someone else's soil & skull, or forcing people to make my language their own.

3.

In *Discipline & Punish*, white French philosopher Michel Foucault offers insight into the culture & structure of the prison, & into the carceral nature of our society. Foucault writes of the omnipresence of power & about how power is exercised in other institutional contexts like schools, the military & hospitals. "Discipline," writes Foucault, "defines each of the relations that the body must have with the object that it manipulates." That is, *discipline* is about controlling the body's movement, making certain ways of being & doing seem impossible. *Discipline* is the regulation of *practice*, a regulation of *methodology*, a regulation of *what* & *how* we *do*, *what* & *how* we *make*.

4.

Whenever I intellectualize what I attempt to do in my own work, I'm haunted by the specter of Carlos Argentino Daneri, the librarian, the poet, the know-it-all from Jorge Luis Borges's short story "The Aleph." The narrator describes Carlos Argentino Daneri as "authoritarian but also unimpressive." Daneri simultaneously recites & shamelessly applauds his own intellectually crafty poetry. "Daneri's real work," suggests the narrator, "lay not in the poetry but in his invention of reasons why the poetry should be admired." Daneri is his own best critic & publicist. I caution against ever becoming as wiggity wack as Daneri; however, I'm certain that my insistent Catholic self-deprecation is merely a variation of Daneriesque self-applause. In any case, you should know, these fears guide my hesitations, & I'm super suspicious of any of us becoming the Carlos Argentino Daneris of our day.

5.

Discipline, for Foucault, is a technology of *power*. Through this definition, an *artist who is disciplined* is *not* someone who demonstrates an unwavering commitment to his or her or their craft; it is *not* someone who, as Dead Prez might suggest, plans his or her or their work & works his or her or their plan. Rather an *artist who is disciplined* is *instead* an artist whose practices may be heavily (self-) regulated due to the demands & desires of *power* & *the powerful*.

6.

During one semester of ninth grade, I learn how to type on an electric typewriter—perhaps one of the most exhilarating moments of my academic career! No longer would I attempt to type my 12-page discourse on indigenous Black people in the Philippines with solely my two index fingers: sixth grade. Nor would I need to beg my mother to type my scientific inquiries into stingray or the chronic obstructive pulmonary disease called *asthma*: fifth grade. I can finally type without taking my eyes off of the paper. I feel I will go far in life. O, the music! One afternoon, the teacher, Mr. Matthews, summons me back into class. He walks me to my workstation & says, "What's this?" It appears as if someone has punched the typewriter in the mouth & its little white keys are scattered all over the floor. "Did you do this? Did you? Tell me. This is unacceptable." What kind of monster does Mr. Matthews think I am? "No," I say. "Well," he says, "you were the last one on this machine. So, I'm sending you to detention. This is unacceptable. I expected better from you." This is the first & only time I am ever sent to detention. So, I cry.

7.

I encountered *creative writing* as a spoken word artist. I was inspired by groups like I Was Born with Two Tongues, 8th Wonder, & Balagtasan Collective, & solo artists such as Saul Williams & Sarah Jones. At that time, for those of us who were learning to reclaim our voices, writing was about immediacy. If there was a protest, we—students, activists & artists—would write poems to articulate our grievances & demands. If we were performing in front of a class, we'd weave in references from our readings & reinterpret the relationship between history & the present. We & our poetics were prepared to fight for social justice at all times. Some of us romanticized ourselves as *cultural workers*. On September 12, 2001, I felt it was my duty to write an anti-war poem, which turned out to be a bad anti-war poem, to call out American hypocrisy & to read it at the local poetry slam in order to indict poets who were now too scared to be *radical*. On this basis, this practice of writing & performance, I applied for MFA creative writing programs. When I got to my MFA program, I unwittingly wrote texts that were a hybrid of poetry, memoir, fiction, rant, & obscure political theory & history. My cohort members would get into debates about whether or not my use of footnotes was distracting. Some of the white students suggested that I get rid of the footnotes. They'd say, "Is there a way to incorporate these notes into the text? Can you contextualize them so you don't need them? Or maybe you can make them endnotes?" My Dominicana homegirl argued that my references to Philippine history helped her understand the relationship between her own history of colonialism & mine. I'm sure she didn't agree with one student's suggestion: To make the footnotes into endnotes on a perforated page that the reader could then tear out from the back of the book. This, to me, would make these obscure histories even more ephemeral & even more easily erasable. Eventually, after sitting through workshop after workshop often debating over the wrong aspects of my writing, & after being told that my writing was so "herky-jerky," & that the performative gesture in my texts was not always pleasurable to read, I scotched writing *experimental* texts & began writing narrative fiction. (Still, I wonder how such *disciplining* affects how I write this here now.) I'm convinced that this forced shift was a result of the racial & cultural politics of form—a mainstream suspicion of the transdisciplinary & performative. Now several years out, I slowly make my way back to the immediacy of a literature I once wrote & spoke in order to survive, a literature I had been taught to disown, a literature from which I snobbishly had distanced myself.

8.

To be very clear, these are not stories of oppression per se. I'm trying to distinguish between *discipline* & *oppression*, between *crying* about it & *dying* because of it, between the *violent* & the *violating*.

9.

Discipline is both violent & violating. Epistemologically. Interpretively. Psychically. Emotionally. Materially. Physically. *Discipline* forecloses possibility. *Discipline* is about the regulation of body, mind, desire. *Discipline* is forcing little brown kids to eat only with their forks. *Discipline* is often what makes even the most "radical" of academics legible to the institution—balloons & flowers & tenure for our critique! In fact, *discipline* helps academics get jobs. *Discipline* helps writers get published. This, I think, is part of its violence. This, I think, is part of its danger for us. We become all too legible for the wrong people. We become consumable through our having been *disciplined*. We become good & *disciplined* colonial subjects. Toward a different gravity, *discipline*: is suspicion: is finger on the trigger: is the follow: is shoot first: is no indictment: is no trial: is justified by law & order: *discipline*. In so many ways, *discipline* is so slowly & so rapidly killing us in America. *Discipline* is what wants Ferguson & Chicago & New York & San Diego & San Bernardino & Los Angeles & Oakland & Detroit & Cleveland & every city & every barrio to stop fighting for our dignity, to stop imagining life, to stop struggling for genuine freedom. In my estimation, this has to do with *discipline* as a technology of power. This is all about the structuring of impossibility, the impossibility of human dignity.

10.

I can't help but wonder if I've been *disciplined* to cite Foucault, & whether or not it matters if I read Foucault *correctly*. Why, still, am I so anxious about misreading Foucault when I have been misread time & time again? *Discipline*, again, is a technology of *power*. *Discipline* is regulation, regulatory power. In *Straight Outta Compton* (2015), despite the film's historical anachronisms—i.e. all-black Dodger fitteds in the late 80s, we get to see both the threat & enactment of *disciplinary* power, of state power. When NWA decides to defy the Detroit Police Chief's warning & proceeds to perform the hell out of "Fuck tha Police," we see *discipline* operate beyond its initial threat. NWA could've chumped out & *not* performed "Fuck tha Police," but they resist the Detroit Police Department's tactics of control & perform the fuck out of "Fuck tha Police." NWA begins the song. Then: Gunshot sounds, which were, according to some, firecrackers set off by the police themselves. The crowd scatters. In the film, NWA is arrested in front of a crowd in some sort of loading dock. In other accounts, NWA is eventually met by the police at their hotel room. Whether we read this as "radical" or not on the part of NWA is beside the point. What's important here is that artistically & politically NWA pushes against the limits of *discipline*. But that *push* itself has its own limitations, & those limitations are, in fact, set by, fuck, *discipline*.

11.

For now, I fashion myself an *interdisciplinary* thinker & artist. Yet, *interdisciplinarity*, too, itself has its limits. Even *interdisciplinarity*—the mixing & sampling of *disciplinary* methods—might be violent & violating. It presupposes that we retain *disciplines, disciplining*. Commenting on the notion of *interdisciplinarity*, badass feminist filmmaker, writer & composer Trinh T. Minh-ha writes: "it is rare to see such a notion stretched to the limits, so that the fences between disciplines are pulled down." Should we bend or pull or stretch or completely dismantle & eat the fences of *discipline*? Perhaps I'm after *anti-disciplinarity*, which needs no justification, which makes me only accountable to my communities & not to any structures of power that need to make sense of what I/you/we have been doing all along anyway. I—

12.

In the most abstract metaphorical terms, I keep banging my head against the limits of *discipline*—I live in the Matrix. I'm fearful that we can't live outside of the matrices of ongoing colonial domination. I say this as it carries with it all kinds of contradictions, i.e. my position as tenure-track professor & as a first-world writer with health benefits & a near-empty checking account. In concrete terms, I'm seeking permissions for writing & making what I write & make, permissions for us to imagine an *un-disciplined*, freer, autonomous life. What keeps me from doing so comfortably & confidently? What of the fact that I still seek permissions? & permissions from what? Permissions from whom?

13.

Where & when & how is it that we've learned to *discipline* our body & imagination?

14.

Where & when & how is it that we have come to do what we do with little or no regard for what has been done to us?

15.

I've arrived at a semi-conclusion: This foray into *discipline* has to do with my anxiety of knowing how to use English, grasping it, standing outside of its capacity to call me names, to call my mama names, its capacity to call you & me its own, its capacity to kill & let die & die & die, its capacity to narrate the impossibility of our futures.

16.

I'm in kindergarten. It's later in the year. Our parents have come to our performance. We, all of us little brown & Black & yellow & red & white kids in pressed flower-print shirts, are dancing our hearts out, with zero regard to settler colonialism, to the hukilau. O, yes, we are so fucking going to the hukilau! I have the choreography down. My hair may be stupid & my movements too rigid & not watery enough. But what matters most is that I'm doing things properly. What matters most is that I know my role. I imagine that right here & right now is the precise moment in which I learn first that *discipline* is about the artist who never ever dares to lay the crayon on its ribs.

You, Praxes for Loving

1. Corporealities

Your thick black hair
is so abject, so tangled,

in bobby pins & hair ties.
You are as precious as

a rice seedling. In your
marrow, are hungry

children who eat boiled
banana. You, on this

train, have a chance
to unweave your tangles.

2. Epistemologies

You are as precious
as a rice seedling—

you know the pain
of intimacy: stone, vein,

ephemeral. You, on this
train, have a chance to

unweave your tangles.
Your legs ache just

before sleep. It feels,
you say, like dying.

3. Ontologies

You know the pain of
intimacy: stone, vein,

ephemeral. You wait for
visions, for the right train

in the wrong station. Your
legs ache. Just before sleep.

It feels, you say, like
dying. My memory,

you say, is what fucks
me up...I remember: Things.

4. Cartographies

You wait for visions. For the
right train in the wrong station.

There are tenement fires in your
blood, your bones wet of Manila.

My memory, you say, is what
fucks me up…I remember:

Things. There are women & lolas
locked in your joints for refusing.

5. Historiographies

There are tenement fires. In your blood.
Your bones wet. Of Manila. You are

the historical moment in which
dandelions hum flame. There are

women. & lolas. Locked. In your
joints. For refusing. Has the wind

from the Pacific rustled through
your leaves? Have I given?

6. Ethnographies

You are the historical moment
in which dandelions hum.

Flame. In. Your. Marrow are. Hungry
children. Who eat boiled banana.

Has the wind from the Pacific rustled
through your leaves? Have I? Given.

Your thick. Black hair. So abject.
So tangled. In bobby pins & hair ties.

The Girl Who Fills Her E's

The Girl Who Fills Her E's is not hypothetical. Perhaps you could say she is nonfictional. & imagined. & real. Perhaps she is. This girl exists indeed. You can tell by her perfect teeth, whiter than crayon shavings, that thick hair, so abject, so tangled, blacker than the blackest tar in the Manila sky, & those lips, created of very nice, very soft, very earthly material. On good days, the girl's laughter materializes worlds for you: Dandelions hum flame & the winds glow. & then all things suggest city—of sizzling eggs, of peachy perfume, of scented candles & citronella smoke. There is no such thing as a bad day.

This girl would say that she herself, the girl, does not exist. You would ask why not, & she, the girl, would simply reply, "I am a woman." This woman exists indeed. Her arms & fingernails are biomythographically long & slender & there are tenement fires in her blood. She is that which is necessary for the wind to glow. Her darkness is this world's.

Rest assured, this woman is really real. She matters. Is matter. Is not a metaphor for perfection. She ignores alarm clocks & changes outfits several times before leaving the house. She cries, too. That thick black hair gets tangled in bobby pins. & her legs ache just before she falls asleep. This woman is not hypothetical. She has nonfictional nightmares & still loves. Still sleeps. Then wakes. Her memory, the woman believes, is what fucks her up. She says that she remembers: Things.

This woman does not conflate love with ideology. She says, Try harder. She asks you what you want. Her ears are soft, her inner ear often suffers infections but still she listens deeply. She is sensitive, as precious as a rice seedling, & she carries darkness whether she likes it or not, whether it's hers or yours or God's. The darkness, she has learned, is.

There is a tiny valley carved into her upper arm. It, too, like her lips, is pleasant to kiss. It, too, knows tragedy, the violence of migration & home. But she, the woman, is far too gorgeous for Melpomene to pay her any bother.

One morning, this woman was a girl. The girl's lola, a teacher with very round & very eager eyes, was teaching the girl how to write. The English alphabet, the girl thought, was ridiculous. The girl called the moon an O, the sun an O, & lola's eyes O's. The girl wondered why letters mattered. If they mattered. In the humidity of Quezon City, in a crowded house, on the concrete, beside the couch, the girl practiced, on a sheet of notebook paper, her letters. She used a black crayon, the shavings piling up around her O's & other letters. She had the most fun with vowels. She said that the letter I was her arms, her teeth, her hair, her lifetimes, her narrative. She'd joke—in Tagalog, she'd think, & in English she'd whisper, "My I's are tangled." She was never confused about E's. She'd first draw the brackets—the top, the bottom & the back. Then, she'd draw-in the lines, more than one. More than several, actually. "That's wrong, anak," her lola once said. "But," said the girl, "if there is only one line, the E might fall. Plus, where would the other lines go? Where would they live? How could they live apart?" The girl didn't care if she was wrong.

It is impossible *not* to fall in love with this woman, this woman who used to be The Girl Who Fills Her E's. Yes: she laughs & makes the winds glow. "Do you think about families?" she once asked. "To me," she said, "groups of pencils, of markers, groups of crayons, groups of anything, were families. I love the idea of the family. I carry them in my joints. Though sometimes, nowadays, I get headaches. My I's get tangled so often." "Your I's?" you asked. "My hair," she said.

This woman, who with a black crayon drew the brackets of an E on a sheet of notebook paper, this woman, the one who proceeded to fill the E with several lines, infinite teeth, the one who after finishing the E peeled it from the paper & began using it to comb out her headaches, is the same woman whose blood is full of tenement fire, whose life is the beauty of trauma, the trauma of beauty, is the same real & imaginable woman for whom you shall forever fall.

For Your Solitudes Crowded with Loneliness: Letter to My Nephew

for Christian Jay Doro

You & I are standing
at the bottom of Grandma's staircase.
There's a Buzz Lightyear figurine
at the edge of a step.
Perhaps Buzz is ready to fly
or *fall with style*.
You are not yet three years old.
You point to Buzz & you say,
"Buzz is sad."
& I say nothing, but
I wonder how you know sadness
so soon. I wonder how you came up
with blaming your cousin
for breaking your heart—
you press your little palm
to your chest & say:

"God put my heart here &
she taked it out & breaked it."

You got mad Buzzes—
every size, every color, the
good one suited in white & lime
& purple, the *evil* twin in purple
& gray, the pudgy one,
the talking one, the one with a laser
that works, the one fastened to a rocket

which is fastened to RC—
Isn't it wonderful how this scene
became the toy?!?
Buzz with a flickering laser,
Buzz with a jammed laser button,
chipped-face blue Buzz that
Grandpa bought in the Philippines,
Buzz with his legs broken off
so he can now fit in the spaceship.

Remember you used to write
your z's backwards: *Buss.*
That's how it sounds
when Grandma says it: "Bhahss."
Then you go ahead &
say something like, "Actually—"
& on that word alone, Grandma lifts you
with all of the wonder in the world
& says over & over:

"Where did you get those word?"

"Where did you get those word?"

"How come you know all those word?"

"Oh my God, totoy—"

"How come you are so good in English?"

"How come you are so good, anak, in English?"

You've got that one-armed Buzz.
This is the Buzz that Mommy fastens
to the ring pillow
at your uncle's wedding
so you're not afraid
to walk down the aisle alone.

You are but four by now &
you already have hair issues.
Perhaps you (*like me*) hate yourself
on bad hair days, which,
for you, & certainly for me,
might be every single day.
You don't want that mohawk
thing anymore—that was for
two-year olds who had
no say in the matter.
You now keep your hair shaggy
& comb it or don't comb it
like the unruly hair of
them white boys on TV.
But you wonder why your hair
is so annoyingly straight
& black & flat & uncooperative
& you wonder why your part
on different days lands
on different hemispheres of your head.
You wonder why you don't have freckles,
why you don't turn red or pink in the sun.
Now you want Phineas hair,
or is it Ferb hair? Is it orange

or green, spiky or flat?

You're still young enough
to let me dab mousse in your hair,
to let me part your hair neatly
with Grandpa's comb.

Later, you ask your cousin,
"Do I look like a nerd?"

You must be five at this point.
You & Auntie are watching
them white kids on Disney again—
Is it *Zack & Cody*? Or the *Wizards
of Waverly Place*? (Oh wait:
Selena Gomez is mestiza.)
Anyway, you turn to Auntie
& instead of saying what you've said before,
that you're tired of always being so small,
you say as you stare at the floor:

"I don't like being brown."

You probably wonder
why your Auntie & I look so lost
& why Auntie decides to make you
tell her who is brown—

"Auntie, Uncle,
Grandma, Grandpa,
Mommy, Daddy, Ate Bella…"

Auntie asks: "Do you think we're ugly?"

Of course not, I hope you say.

But you simply say, "No."

& stare at the floor as if
you're thinking about
disappearing or flying far far away.

You now make it a point to tell Auntie
that you like Dora because she's brown
& that you like Princess Tiana
because she's brown, too—
you can call her *Black*, it's okay.

You're in kindergarten & first grade
& second grade & you're reading
everything in sight & asking me
if you're pronouncing things correctly:
"Is that Onion Bank or Union Bank?"

You no longer rock two different shoes
to make yourself look faster like The Flash
& you no longer style only one side
of your hair & call yourself Two Face.

So much has happened by now &
you've seen holes in your bedroom walls
the way I used to see holes
in my bedroom walls. & you most likely

feel like your insides are falling & spilling
whenever there are people around
& you most likely feel like your insides are
falling & spilling whenever there is
yelling or crying in the house.

Remember when Shrek got mad
on the Christmas DVD & you hid
behind the couch, then bolted upstairs?

Auntie & I think you're so smart
& so creative & so sensitive & so caring.

Remember the time you tricked Auntie?

You must have been four.

You were hiding behind a pillow
& you kept saying:

"You know what I am! You know what I am!"

"A ghost?" said Auntie.

"No," you said.

Then you kept saying:

"You know what I am! You know what I am!"

"A monster?"

"No," you said, "I'm a pillow."

We trust you'll be okay.

You're seven now
& it's the first time
Auntie & I take you to school.
You don't want to be there
but you know you have to.
You hug us. You kiss us.
Then you walk across the blacktop.
Your Spiderman backpack
is way too big—it swings from
side to side & throws off your step.

Auntie turns to me & says:

"It must be tough being a parent...
you just hope your kid will be okay."

You toss your backpack in a pile & wander off.

You are smaller than all of the other kids.
Your jeans are too long—
you fold them with big folds.
You tiptoe across the blacktop.
You're looking for someone.
You're looking for something.

I tell your Auntie that you're looking
for your homies.

No kid on the basketball court asks you to play—
but that's okay, you don't play sports.

So you find nothing.

So you find nobody.

So you walk back
to where your class lines up.

You stand at the periphery
of a 4-square game & none
of them kids invite you to play either.
They don't even acknowledge you.

(*I hate them all.*)

You go to the other side of the handball wall

& you just sit—crisscross applesauce—on the asphalt.

You rest your cheeks in your hands.

You watch the other kids have fun together.

& you wait for the whistle to blow.

"This," says Auntie, "looks like a routine."

The sky is no longer gray
& the sun is out from hiding

& I have no idea
what to say to you.

I have no idea how
to make the spilt feelings
of our insides go away.

Do you have those spilt feelings inside?

You are thinking & thinking
& I am thinking & thinking:

I know the feeling,
I know the feeling.

I wish we were elsewhere again.   (~~Fuck~~ ~~Damn~~ *Darn this school.*)
I wish we were elsewhere again
& the whistle would never blow.

I wish we were elsewhere,
on a different day, not a school day.
& I'm dabbing mousse in your hair,
& you're drawing the maddest & saddest
of faces, their arms & legs sprouting from
their heads—*where are their bodies?*
& you're spelling & spelling
English words for Grandma.

I wish we were elsewhere,
sometime before today,
that one time when…

You pull Auntie aside
& you tell her you have a secret.

"What is it?" she says.

& it's a secret that nobody knows,
that nobody *can* know, especially your cousin.

(*I'm truly sorry that I do know.*)

It's a secret I imagine makes you feel
full & good inside.

Perhaps it's a feeling that is better than
the feelings you have at school.

You're ready to tell Auntie your secret.

She bends down to hear you

& you whisper:

"I like unicorns."

The Bluest Rage Tonight

a meditation for Stanley "Tookie" Williams (1953-2005)

Redlands, California, 1989. We live on Brookside Avenue, where
peewees pack heat—weak .22s, home of brown & yellow & Black &
some poor white pipsqueaks who Royal Rumble, who play tackle
football on lawns littered with dog shit, who play Homerun Derby
with tennis balls on a tennis court, who play American Gladiator &
hurl clumps of mud at each other, who play make-believe crips &
make-believe bloods (not cops, not robbers) & pull plastic shotguns
& revolvers on each other. Where it smells of goat bile soup. & sewage.
& Old English 800. & Hamburger Helper. & bean tostadas. & fried pork
innards. & weed. & Ritz crackers & bologna & American cheese. &
kimchi. I've been hiding underneath my Superman blanket, atop my
race car bed, waiting & waiting like God. I finally go outside & run
into Clap. Clap is mad bony. & lanky & tall. Clap's girlfriend, I think,
lives upstairs. Clap smells of Cool Water. He rocks ill-fitting khakis
& loosely-laced British Knights. He's got a mad maddog. & he folds
a blue handkerchief—the kind farmers use to cover their mouths—
& hangs it from his back pocket. My older brother's homies call Clap
a "crab" because Clap wears so much "crab-ass blue." I wonder if
it's because Clap thinks he's the ocean, or the sky, or that he belongs
there. In the ocean. Or the sky. Clap turns to me & says, "What up,
cuz?" My T-shirt is mostly gray, but the UNLV logo on my chest is
blood-ass red. Later, I learn that, at the park across the street, Patrick
& another one of my brother's homies beat Clap silly with a wooden
baseball bat.

Still Redlands, 1991. My brother says we should wait to see *Boyz n the Hood* because the movie theater is the latest war zone: bloods on the screen, blood on the carpet, the blood of youth, messianic blood: eulogies waiting. Several weeks pass & we finally watch the movie in an empty theater near Fiesta Village. I'm not sure if I'm sad for Ricky or Doughboy, or the fact that we have known & loved & worried about both the Rickys & Doughboys of the world. I leave my blood-red Chicago Bulls jacket in the closet whenever we pass the projects. I'm upset because my brother put an 8-ball sticker on the rear bumper of his red Honda Prelude. "You're only nine," he says as onlookers flash signs at us. "Stop fucking crying."

Oceanside, California, 1994. At 13, if you're not making out with someone, you best stay home, or let the peewees or BGs jump you in. Frank Rock, that goofy-looking kid with the ill uprocking skills, & decent though inconsistent basketball handles, the one with clean-ass black Reebok classics, decides that breakdancing can't protect him. Before school, at the bus stop, Rashad jumps Frank Rock in to a crip set. Rashad punches Frank Rock in the throat. Frank Rock's throat hurts. We board the bus. At lunch, Frank Rock kicks it with the crips, but he & I still exchange nods when we pass each other. Weeks later, one day, after school, off the bus, in the middle of the street, Rashad jumps Frank Rock out. They shake hands. They give each other dap. Frank Rock is not a crip. Again. I never get jumped in. Or out. Frank Rock continues to hold his throat.

Oceanside, 1996. My friend Junior says some "crabs from outta town" dragged him into a van & beat his ass. Junior says the crips were twenty-something. "Stupid motherfuckers," Junior says, "fucking with sixteen-year-olds." Junior's eyes are bloodshot. Red, his aspirations. In this city, to bloods & wannabe bloods *Black* means *crab* & *crab* means *enemy*. To crips & wannabe crips *Samoan* means *slob*, & *Filipino* means *slob*, *slob* most certainly means enemy. This poor white boy, a self-proclaimed blood with freckles & an earring, claims to have been bangin since the second grade. I, for one, don't believe him. I do, however, believe in my friends who used to play 21 on our driveway—Tre, Jeremiah, Carlos…But things have changed. Tre throws down with Kenny on the bus because Kenny proclaims to be a blood, & Tre, a crip, or, to Kenny, a *crab*, calls Kenny a *slob*. Tre swings at Kenny with his 3-ring binder. There is now a cut, red, just below Kenny's eye.

Plaza Bonita Mall, National City, California, 1997. I make it point *not* to wear anything that would bring attention to myself. Yet still, somehow, a mob of Laotian kids roll up on me & my homies. "Why," a pudgy one asks, "you eyein my boy for, blood?" I tell the pudgy one that I don't bang. & then the pudgy one proceeds to rep his set. Over & over again. He keeps talking to me & asking me what I'm looking at. His fists clenched. His step misdirected.

Lourdes Restaurant, National City, California, 2002. We're college kids, the lucky ones who "made it," some from Vallejo, some from San Diego, me from Oceanside, some from Los Angeles, some from Anaheim. We're eating different textures of fried pork & talking about how this restaurant resembles a karaoke bar one would find in Manila— all kinds of mirrors, chrome & banana leaves. A drunk Filipino dude, maybe in his 30s, red-faced as fuck, leans over to me. "Ey," he says, "What group are you?" I say, "I don't bang, homie." I can tell he wants to fight. He presses on: "What group are you?" I'm clenching my fork. I tell my friend next to me that I'm gonna stab this motherfucker with my fork if he starts anything. "Homie," I repeat, "I don't bang." This dude says, "Oh…I bang….I bang." He pounds his chest & reaffirms: "Okay, Man…I…I Bang." I wait for him to rep his set. For him to hear himself. Over & over again. Perhaps, over & over again, no one has ever heard him. Just because I want to stab this dude with my fork doesn't mean that I don't care whether or not he lives or dies when it's his turn to get caught slippin.

Oakland, California, 2005. I often, so very very often, hear things like, "My bad, blood." Or, "Ey, blood, I'm comin through on BART right now, blood. I'm at Fruitvale, blood." Or, "Ey, blood, you got the time?" & the connection is more than veins, more than ephemerality, more than a mere city, The Town. What I hear is not that different from what Clap had said to me: "What up, cuz?" What up, Cousin, Family, Estranged.

Oakland, California, December 12, 2005, 11:24PM. I'm watching the news. So many young people waiting outside of San Quentin. A candlelight vigil. A million prayers. For a phone call. Waiting for a miracle. Sympathy from the Governator. I'm wondering why I can't get myself to drive to San Quentin. I'm wondering why I can't convince myself that peace is possible. I'm wondering if my heart will ever stop racing whenever I'm strolling through the streets of Oakland, Richmond, San Francisco, Oceanside, San Diego, National City, Long Beach, Los Angeles, wherever, & I catch myself wearing the wrong red or the wrong blue. & I catch myself clenching my fork. Tonight, Tookie Williams awaits peace on death row. Tonight, bloods & crips & families continue to mourn. & I realize that this cannot be about *peace*—for peace is forever & ever so goddamn elusive. This has to be about *the promise of* peace, the promise of letting our hair down a little, just for a few moments, the promise of letting our locks & braids turn gray, into ash, into memory, into air, into prayer, the promise of what Tookie Williams's life means tonight & forever & ever & ever.

But Life Goes On

I wonder if you, too, had mad rage & longing as a youngster & if you, too, found in listening to Tupac a way to stare at the world through your rearview & scream to God.

I wonder if you, too, think about when your Filipina immigrant mama said to you, "I like that Tupac because he *love* his mom."

I wonder if you, too, oiled & sharpened the blades of your Wahl clippers & shaved your own head every three days, rocked cheap sterling silver chains & bracelets & clean black T's, & along with your cousins & older brothers you described such looks as being *Pac'd out*.

I wonder if you cried when you heard Tupac got shot again, when you heard he'd lost a lung, when you heard he didn't make it this time.

I wonder if you mourned that morning by calling the same pager of some anonymous vocalist just to hear over & over again a voicemail greeting—*what a beautiful elegy that was for Tupac Amaru Shakur!*

I wonder if it still upsets you when people claim that Tupac is alive.

I wonder if you, too, are suspicious of Tupac's posthumous fanbase.

I wonder if you, too, are a little convinced that Tupac is like Jesus. Or if you, too, only started listening to Biggie & Nas & Jay Z a couple of years after Pac's death, when you felt less guilty about it.

(Do you, too, wonder which young rappers today could hold their own in the presence of Pac?)

How did you feel about the hologram at Coachella?

How do you feel now every time a new album drops?

Have you stopped listening?

Did you, too, want to punch that music grad student TA who in your hip hop class said some stupid shit like, "Basically, I can't think of anything positive about Tupac other than the fact that his mother was a Black Panther"?

I wonder if you, too, remain perplexed & stuck about your approximation of Black masculinities, your desire to know them, your romanticizing of them, your appropriation of a commodified form of them, your privilege of not being Black in America.

Despite this, are you, too, committed to thinking deeply about why Pac could mean so much to you & yours?

Are you committed to naming his fire in your own veins?

Because regardless of the critical theories & realities of race & social & physical death, regardless of his Blackness & your brownness, Pac has influence in your life.

& what of *Tupac: Resurrection*? Were you floored or freaked the fuck out by the ways in which they spliced up disparate & disjunctive interviews? Do Pac's speeches & interviews still get you? Are they still *that* revolutionary for you? Do they conjure up the Marxist in you? The ya basta in you?

You, too, might wonder & wonder so badly why Tupac lives in your life.

You, too, don't want to idolize him, or commodify his memory, or trap him in nostalgia, or fetishize his pain, or make him a theory, or a theme for #ThrowbackThursday.

You, too, never wanna forget that Tupac was real *for real.*

Perhaps you shuffle through Pac's ridiculously extensive discography in hopes of being back in the day again.

Do you, too, mourn the dead by wondering & listening: how many brothers & sisters fell victim to the streets?

Perhaps you, too, simply want to be as hungry & prolific as Tupac was.

You, too, might wanna fight for a different world, a world so profoundly & fundamentally different from the one in which you & Tupac grew up, the one in which you lived on & he died.

So, what is stopping you?

Stranger Here: Oral History (*U.S. v. Narciso & Perez*)

Leonora M. Perez (1944 –)

I was a small kid before & I play & I like to be a nurse & I get those dragonfly you know that one anak & I get my needle & I inject them with water then my sister says why do you do that I said because I want to be a nurse one of these days I will gonna be one they're so neat their white clothes uniform shoes cap & all those I think they don't die because they're so nice & so clean they don't die because they're helping people I told Tatay you have to send me to school one thing is the only way I can see America is to be a nurse Tatay said no you can't go because they killed those nurse in Chicago that was Speck in that time when I leave home to come here Nanay & Tatay is crying & crying Tatay said if you find a nice

guy marry him you're getting old when I arrive America it's too far it's
another world hindi maganda ang America I'm lonely I have no friends
I work nights then I meet your dad everyone said you have a partner
now for the Valentine's it's a dance in the hospital I said who is that your dad
said oh you're going then we're all going then we dance & dance & later on

then I know him he calls me he come to the house we were boyfriends for six months we go out we take the train then he said if you want me then I'll stay if you don't marry me I go to Japan with my brother but if I stay we'll continue if not then we don't know that time your dad he work in St. Francis in the laundry department he said if you like me then we just get married if not then maybe I'm not coming back I go home after Japan so I said okay then when it was a big wedding our invitation is made in the Philippines we had the reception in a Chinese restaurant that was a nice love story huh & then time goes on & on & then why did those thing happen god I thought America was really a milk & honey I was so depress here I am provinciana poor as mud I come for greener pasture & then those thing happen we did not do those crime okay hold okay hold na okay let me tell you what happen what really happen anak I work in Ann Arbor VA in Michigan in ICU okay okay every time there's code in the hospital an ICU nurse has to come to bring the cut-down tray of course we gonna do that because that's our job di ba in that time in whatever floor there's a code how come it's all the time something is happening di ba how come they're all dying maybe it's anesthesia in ER maybe it's too hot maybe no air-con then one night on August fifteen nineteen seventy-five the date we have three code in ICU three code one after the other one stop

breathing we don't know if it's heart or respiratory or what it's code blue
then we're not done with this one & there's another coding here o God
could you imagine that night we got it settled after work we were so so
tired & then they said they wanted to talk to me downstairs I said who
they said the FBI I'm afraid because that's FBI we're just a stranger here

we don't speak the language how can we express our self how can we explain what we want to say if we don't know how to say those FBI always ask & ask did you administer that medicine I said no then they say just admit it was your friend the other Filipino nurse I said no she didn't do anything & then this goes on & on & then one day June sixteen nineteen seventy-six the date I was working morning something fishy like I have hunch something happening I was walking in the street & two big men was all of a sudden holding me they said you are under arrest for the crimes you did in Michigan I said I didn't do anything what crime I didn't do any crime & they said follow us to the car or we will drag you we arrested your friend too I said you don't even read my rights then they cover my handcuff with my sweater I don't know it's crazy those FBI your dad he wait for me in the train & suddenly I'm in T.V. all over the place I want to let the world to know why did those thing happen we're innocent we're being discriminated even if I am just immigrant even if I am just stranger here I'm a human being di ba even if I am just immigrant here I'm a human being di ba even if I am just stranger here I'm a human being di ba even if I am just immigrant here I'm a human being di ba even if I am just stranger here I'm a human being di ba even if I am just immigrant here I'm a human being di ba

Leonora, archive of: Film Transcripts

A. Fundraising T-Shirt, Orange, Thinning, Some Holes, Graphic: Stencil of F. B. Narciso & L. M. Perez, Text Reads: (Top) Support VA Nurses (Bottom) Stop FBI Frame-Ups, 1977.

LEONORA M. PEREZ: this shirt was made by the support group of the VA nurses in support for us for the fundraising that they did in Michigan during that case I didn't know they did this when I saw it I went to the flea market & everybody was selling this for five dollars in support for us & the funds went into the the Narciso-Perez fund defense fund & they sold this there & I didn't know they did this & then said oh I have my face there & then they gave me one that was uh after we were convicted we were doing maybe not I can't remember now if it's after or before because we're getting support for from all the people when I see it now I couldn't believe that you know one of those days I will be in this you know in this kind of shirt & then being you know advertise in U.S. you know United States you know very big country I kept this for so long so it will be one of my souvenirs so when you know when I grow old & I'm already gone my children can I can pass it to my children & there's a story to it

B. *Photograph, Black & White, Outside of Courthouse in Detroit, Michigan, Depicted: L. M. Perez, E. A. Perez, Jr., M. C. Magabo, A. Magabo, 1977.*

LEONORA M. PEREZ: okay this photograph was taken I think June fourteen nineteen seventy-seven or June twenty nine nineteen uh I cannot remember the exact date but this is in front of the federal court in Detroit on the picture is my husband Epifanio Perez, Jr. Nanay Maxima Castillo Magabo & my dad Anacleto Magabo you can see what I was wearing on this I was the one who sewed that & also on Nanay's jacket I learned how to sew because I was so bored I had no job after the trial in the morning I go home I have nothing to do so I just learn how to sew & every time I go to the court I have a new dress new coat because I sew it at night Nanay & Tatay they were worried when they're coming because they cannot they said how can we go there when Leonie cannot pick us up she's in jail Nanay thought I was still in jail & she said we can't remember Jun's face yeah & after that they came over & we pick them up in the airport Nanay & Tatay was surprised because I was there & I was not in jail & they were happy you know to see us Tatay said what hah they were crying he said what happen I said I don't know they just got me I said I am innocent I didn't do anything & Tatay said oh I should just just just why are you the one going I should just go to jail for you your dad he cried when I when they arrested me he didn't know that I got arrested he was coming home from work we will meet in the babysitter in Chicago because we drop your brother off in the babysitter I take the he I take train going to the VA & then Dad drives to his work & then when we go home I take the train & stop there & we meet there & then we go home to Evanston & that time I did not arrive your Dad he was waiting & waiting I did not come he they went home him & your brother & my friend called her him he said oh don't wait for Leonie he she's arrested she's now in the county jail in Chicago your brother saw me in TV the five o' clock news he said that's my mom with the FBI but the night before your brother was playing cop & he tries to handcuff me all the time & he said you're guilty oh yeah he was doing that because you know how loko loko your brother is he he played cop & he said I am the FBI I'm gonna get you then he see me in T.V. & said that I hate that man he said to that big FBI Russo & Gunther yeah he said I hate that he got my mom & that was already flashing in Chicago because they got us already & they said two nurses indicted only God knows you know we're innocent even if the people say we're guilty I I we we did not do anything

C. Crocheted Blanket, Green & Cream, Zig Zag Pattern, Note: Made in the Federal Prison Camp in Alderson, West Virginia, 1977.

LEONORA M. PEREZ: just testing it okay we gonna start now what do you wanna know everything or nothing okay crochet croche-ted crocheted croche-ted what is it crocheted blanket how did I have this okay I was interested doing this because I met a friend there in jail she has been there a long time she had seniority she has a nice room that's where I learn how to crochet this because she's too busy & I saw it & this is nice & I said why don't you I I will just do that I'll just copy it & keep myself busy because PI said she wanna keep herself busy by playing volleyball she played with the inmates I did not play I was the scorer every time she goes play I go with her & I was carrying this one crocheting oh ah the federal prison is all the way where the trees are all barb wires it's surrounded with fences & then when we check in all the inmates were looking at us because it was on the news that the two nurses who were convicted will be sent to Federal Prison in West Virginia so when we arrive all of them are looking at us they were in the living room they said oh you are the nurses who killed those patients how many did you kill yeah that is how they ask PI they ask me so we did not say anything we just went in I was so nervous I was so afraid I don't know what to do a lot of people then they uh we had to do the examination like to check-in mug shots you know uh check everything your shoes everything you're naked you go take a shower naked both of us me & PI take your picture after you shower & it's all mug shot it's all ugly & then you face the camera they take the picture & then they showed us our room they said you guys can have a nice room here if you've been here a long time & we said no sir we don't plan to stay here & we don't want any seniority in this place we wanna go out we wanna go home tomorrow we don't wanna stay here I kept the blanket because it's my souvenir & also it's very you know historical for me this is this is my comfort you know

Phenomenology of Superhero

in response to the Superhero Portrait Invitational (2015) at Modern Eden Gallery, San Francisco, CA

1.

Supposedly, it's 1983. But since I'm certain that I'm at least three years old, I'll say for now, that it's 1984. & I'm three years old. & my hair, similar to Astro Boy's, even though I've never ever watched Astro Boy, has not decided what it wants to do in & for this world. Astro Boy's hair is flat & round & spiky & black & widow's peak. My own hair is long & short & black & straight & tangled & thin & bangs & wings & stupid uneven, jagged bangs & two pesky cowlicks & it smells of apple juice & Aqua Net. I can't even. My skin is very dried. & pink brown. Very eczema & scab. Very peeled. I'm sharing the passenger's seat with my mother. My two older brothers sit on the floor behind us. My father, in the driver's seat. We're a young migrant family. In a gutted royal blue GMC conversion van. We're parked somewhere in the unbearably hot desert. It's nighttime. There are stars. (It's just Las Vegas.) Hanging from the driver's side window is a weighty metal speaker. The weighty metal speaker is a fading gold. It crackles. It cuts out from time to time. We're at the drive-in movie theatre. My mother has packed spam, rice & soft drink. We're watching *Superman III*. & although I'm captivated by the young Christopher Reeve's stellar performance, not as Superman, but as Clark Kent, I will, years later, appreciate what Richard Pryor, the Black villain computer nerd named Gus, has to offer as far as embodying an implicit though subversive interstellar racial critique. & although I'll later appreciate Richard Pryor for his many gifts, & later be so sad & so heartbroken about Christopher Reeve being thrown from a horse, I'll certainly appreciate, & certainly we'll all appreciate, that in 1993, Superman is played by the handsome Dean Cain, the real-life hapa, born Dean *Tanaka*, the one who played the sweet &

responsible American named Rick with whom fake-French-accent-having Brenda Walsh (of the wholesome Minnesotan 90210-transplanted Walsh family) falls in love while studying abroad in Paris with her friend, Donna Martin, who, despite being mad turnt at her high school prom, did, as a result of spontaneous & committed & coalitional activism, graduate from West Beverly.

2.

I stand. At this podium. This podium stands. At me, I think. This podium is *that* about which I do not give a *fuck*. & I am *that* about which this podium does give a little *fuck*, for I do with *it*, the podium, something *it* cannot do with *me*, the not-podium. *I*, the not-podium orient *it*, the podium. I, the not-podium, imbue *it*, the podium, a function, a purpose. Unless *it* standing right *here* first orients *me*. In any case, I am a failed phenomenologist. I, I think, fail to demonstrate what I should be demonstrating—a Husserlian obsession with the table. &/or this podium. I think. I fail to demonstrate a Husserlian obsession with *what*, i.e. object, is in front of *me*, i.e. subject. Or, am I *subject* actually *object* here now?

3.

Let's say it's 1988. & you're savvy with almost every aspect of popular white heteronormative masculinity, a popular white heteronormative masculinity that is, at its core, kid-friendly. You watch WWF. You believe it is real. You love Randy Macho Man Savage because you yourself have persistently been historicized as *savage*. & you love that fat & round & pasty & mean-mugging & black onesie-spandex-sporting King Kong Bundy because your older cousin's first tag name, his first placas, is *Bundy One*, & King Kong, well…it's fucking King Kong! But you love love love, most of all, Hulk Hogan, the working-class real American, who, at this time, isn't *that* racist. You make it a point to draw Hulk Hogan whenever you draw anything. Whenever you draw anything & anything is always Hulk Hogan, you draw-in Hulk Hogan's mustache so thick that Hulk Hogan becomes *Jesus*. & so then you draw wings on what would've been Hulk Hogan, wings on what is now *Jesus*, which is yet another signifier of what you are not, what you cannot be, what part of you wishes to be, if only for protection, yet another signifier of popular white heteronormative masculinity. You have an abundance of rubber wrestling figures, at least two Hulk Hogans. You have even more G.I. Joes. The plastic kind whose spines are rubber bands & whose joints are tiny little screws. But wait! Never have these G.I. Joes waged international war on the black Cobra Commander. Never have these G.I. Joes been deployed, in your imagination, to fight communism or terrorism. No. These G.I. Joes instead get lined-up against the wall, hands locked behind their heads. Some stand. Some kneel. Which one has the crack rock? Which one threw a stone at the patrol car? You designate one G.I. Joe the police officer. Stopping & frisking, the good old (& new) days. This year, 1988, the movie *Colors* is released. In *Colors*, Sean Penn plays the young studly pig Pacman, not Pacman Manny Pacman, the tragic though heterosexist hero of your later years, but the rookie pig Pacman who chases down bloods, crips & eses, one of whom you swear is really a redheaded white dude with sleepy eyes & one of whom, the one named Larry, is Black. A Black ese, a Black vato, who probably, now that you think about it, is Afro-Latino. From your mama's alarm clock radio, you bump the hell out of Ice-T's song from the *Colors* soundtrack & you rap along, "the nightmare walkin, psychopath talkin, king of the jungle..." This is the soundtrack to your make-believe. These are the scenes of your G.I. Joes, the real American heroes. If your G.I. Joes, however, are profiled gangsters, then can they be your heroes? Which ones are your heroes? Which ones are your superheroes? If your G.I. Joes are not being called to war, what wars do they wage? These no longer seem like questions of phenomenology. Is this, then, an *epistemology* of superhero? Is this, then, about how you have come to un-know or de-know popular white heteronormative masculinity & supplant it with something much more familiar, something much more akin to your oldest brother's homies being gunned down at the nearby park at which you play baseball?

4.

Now I'm no art critic, but the rendition of Wolverine in this exhibition, the Wolverine with bulging traps & eight-pack abs, the one standing against a black backdrop, the one suffering three long bloody wounds, the Wolverine upon which a soft confetti of pink, white & blue flower petals fall....I got two words, which combined, form one effectively motivating hashtag: *#FITSPO*.

5.

This podium stands. I stand among: art, portraits, superheroes. In *Queer Phenomenology: Orientations, Objects, Others*, scholar Sara Ahmed suggests that knowing & being & encountering are not solely about that which exists in front of us. Sara Ahmed suggests that we must attend to what is behind, to that which is in the background. "So," writes Sara Ahmed, "if phenomenology is to attend to the background, it might to do so by giving account of the conditions of emergence for something, which would not necessarily be available in how that thing presents itself to consciousness." What, then, are the 'conditions of emergence' of *me*? Of *you*? Of *us*? Of these superheroes? Of *superhero* itself?

6.

I'm gonna go ahead & say it: Storm in *The Storm Begins*—in her big & wavy silver locks & deep silver eyes & electrified palms—is just as fly & sexy as the non-hit wonder Halle Berry-as-Storm. I'll also go ahead

& say that the Storm in this exhibition appears to be racially ambiguous. To say such a thing, that this depiction of Storm is racially ambiguous, I understand, potentially reifies racialized & colonial understandings of what is fly & what is sexy. I've also expressed that Dean Tanaka, the hapa, is a pretty man. Nevertheless, I've said such things. At this podium.

7.

Dear Talented Portrayer of Aquaman,

You make Aquaman: Aqua-Do-Not-Fucks-with-Me. Your Aquaman emerges from such an utter darkness, which I assume is the sea. & he appears to have no eyes, just abysses within which I get lost & drown. Can I ask you an honest question though? I know nothing about Aquaman. But when my nephew—the one who really wanted my thinning & faded & ratty & almost transparent Superman blanket that I've had since that 1984 evening at the drive-in—was about eight years old, he's ten now, he told me that Aquaman was the wackest, most useless superhero. "What power," asked my nephew, "does Aquaman possess?" My nephew conceded, "Aquaman can summon sharks. But what good is *that* when we're on land?"

8.

"What," I once asked God, "is the opposite of superhero? Villain?"

"No," said God godly, "Filipino."

9.

It is not during the early stages of your life, it is not during the years you use to swim a lot & smell a lot like chlorine & asthma, or the years you used to use your neighbor's bendy Freddy Kruger claws as Wolverine claws. It is today. & every day. & every month. & every year of your standing, your being. Here. On this earth. Oriented toward the world, oriented perhaps toward the Orient, perhaps the Occident, other worlds, the worlds of Others, oriented toward other artists. Why, you ask the artists today, namely the artists who've re-captured & re-signified the verve & musculature of Wonder Woman & Rogue & Cyclops & Thor & even the elastic & slender Catwoman cradling a dead fish, why, you ask, did you not cast *me* as the model for these portraits? You believe that you are much more realistic, that your body type is one to celebrate, that your body type shouldn't be pigeonholed, it shouldn't serve solely as the model that inspired the pudgy (yet fierce & brilliantly rendered) Mighty Mouse.

10.

We, & the objects around us, & art objects in our heads, of our bodies, are shaped by what Sara Ahmed calls our "multiple histories of arrival." We think, we body. We have come. From somewhere, something. & that is the matter of our encounter. Forget the podium. Forget the table. The Object. Forget the furniture.

11.

"A queer furnishing," argues Ahmed, "might be about making what is in the background, what is behind us, more available as 'things' to 'do' things with." If I were to be completely honest about the worth of my art, about what I wished you would *do* with this seemingly ephemeral *thing*, my written response to these *things*, I'd say that I'd like you to purchase this limited first-print manuscript for $31,080, which is the sum total of the remaining works of this exhibition the last time I checked. Okay, I'll also take nothing less than $900—my nephew would never respect me if I couldn't outsell Aquaman. Okay, I'll take $500 & a hug.

12.

I'd like to know if Robert Downey, Jr.'s jerk-face attitude has affected whether or not any participating artists wanted to send in their rendition of Iron Man. & whether or not that precluded any attempt to render James Rhodes, who fortunately for everyone is now played by the king Don Cheadle, who also plays the technology-infatuated porn star Buck Swope in *Boogie Nights*, who eventually finds himself in a donut shop that is being robbed—his white suit & face splattered with blood, brown bag of cash in his hands. Don Cheadle, you should know, was also in the 1988 movie, *Colors*, in which he played Rocket, leader of the crips who rocks his plaid long-sleeve shirt with only the top button fastened, which, to me, is silly & potentially a dramaturgical oversight because, I think, & I'm almost certain, that only the vatos rocked it like that. These days, I watch Don Cheadle as Marty Kaan in *House of Lies*. Marty Kaan is so awesome that he makes me want to be a capitalist. (Okay, I'll sell this manuscript for $400.) In *House of Lies*, after a few seasons of well-narrated tension, Marty Kaan has sex & soon after has a child with the character Jeannie Van Der Hooven, who is played by the talented Kristen Bell, who is also Veronica Mars, but who is also the voice of Anna, the little sister in *Frozen*, an instant Disney classic that is adored by my three-year-old niece, & me, us, whose heroines are the Rapunzels of the world—I'm a fan of Mandy Moore, the voice of Rapunzel, who as Anna's & Elsa's cousin makes a cameo on Queen Elsa's coronation day in *Frozen*—these, all of these, we adore: these signifiers of a popular white heteronormative femininity, which, too, is the opposite of Filipina/o/x. I think, I body.

What Saddens Sardines: A Romantic Outcry

The Person I Love Most often wears slippers in the summertime. Sometimes the slippers are made of worn leather. Sometimes they clap her soles. & sometimes they are just as brown as her. Her feet look powerful, but no one knows how powerful, how timeless. Her slender toes are slender toes. They're immeasurable. Yet, this time is not summertime. It's another season. I can't tell which one. It never matters. Nowadays, nothing does. Her powerful & timeless feet hide in thin socks. The night is warm. We, the Person I Love Most & I, are in San Diego, in a hill town, in a suburb, this is Mira Mesa, in a tract house, in a heptagonal room with chalky green walls, on a carpet hardened with drippings of country white paint, on a long strip of masking paper. We're holding each other. She's upset about something. I should know why. But I don't. Beside us: a dried paint-roller, a roll of blue tape. The Person I Love Most picks up the paint-roller & begins to rattle it against the chalky green walls, coloring the chalky green walls green, a lighter & shinier shade. "It occurs to me," I say to the Person I Love Most, "that you are far away." The Person I Love Most scoots beyond my reach. She is now kneeling in front of the narrowest of the seven walls. With the paint-roller, she pounds at the wall as if it had the face of a disloyal friend, splattering lighter & shinier green & green everywhere. "I'm tired," she says. The Person I Love Most has special hair. It's thick & black & a little tangled. Certainly unquestionable. It knows history. It knows more than it can bear. The Person I Love Most doesn't get haircuts. She refuses to style her hair because she refuses to forget. Angels live in there. Good & bad. & they all love each other from time to time. She doesn't comb. She doesn't brush. She doesn't pick. She lets her hair down to dry, hoping that nothing escapes. She likes & loses bobby pins & hair ties. She gets headaches. She scratches her scalp. "You have to let me in," I say. "It occurs to me that you are far away."

The Person I Love Most says nothing. Then she says, "Nothing." The masking paper rustles as I join The Person I Love Most in painting. My lines are crooked, her lines calculated. Then jagged. Then she stops & no longer cares for painting green walls green. She taps her nose repeatedly with her index finger & leans into me. I cup her elbows gently. Sometimes she hates when things get stuck in her head. Like colors. Or song lyrics. Or the psychologies & traumas of her loved ones. This time something enormous has trapped itself inside of her head. Perhaps it is a history inside of her joints. I think it's *love*. The Person I Love Most obsesses over *love*. Actually, she concentrates on leaving. Not leaving me. Not leaving the world. Or her family. Or her Lola. Or her corgi. O, how she loves loves loves that tricolored corgi named Frankie! The Person I Love Most wants to leave herself sometimes. She, The Person I Love Most, is alchemy herself.

"What's this?" I ask & point to the perfectly round valley of a scar on her upper arm. "My birthmark," she says. "It doesn't look like a birthmark," I say. "It is," she defends. "It's perfect," I say. "It's the Philippines," she says. I believe her. "That's the exact birthmark," I say, "that I've been searching for my entire life."

The first time I heard The Person I Love Most's actual name was in a theatre. It was nearly empty. The seat cushions were wine red & the dancers on stage were lost brown. It was cold. There were echoes. The only thing special about the theatre was The Person I Love Most's posture. The Person I Love Most's posture was perfect, not too rigid & not slouched, but prepared. She was prepared.

We, The First Woman I've Ever Truthfully & Wholeheartedly Loved, who was previously referred to as The Person I Love Most, & I, sit on or in or about a gray or grey concrete stairwell. I, on the top step, & she, three steps below. It is dark. The moon is forgetful. Crickets sound like crickets. It's chilly. So I offer The First Woman I've Ever Truthfully & Wholeheartedly Loved my V-neck sweater. "Impressive," she says. "I'm impressed. Very soft." Yes, I think. She wraps the sweater around her neck. One sleeve hangs off of her shoulder. She cares for the asymmetrical. The First Woman I've Ever Truthfully & Wholeheartedly Loved hides in her hoodie. Her special & thick & black & tangled & unquestionable hair is un-hideable. She's lovely. We're in the right place, outside of her apartment, away from alarm clocks, away from boy-crazy roommates & their crazy boyfriends. We're ready. Alone. I type poems on my old Remington typewriter. It weighs more than The First Woman I've Ever Truthfully & Wholeheartedly Loved. I'd rather The First Woman I've Ever Truthfully & Wholeheartedly Loved sit closer. The Remington is an iron black—the letters on the keys are faded. When I hit each key, letters sledgehammer themselves onto paper. "My poems," I say, "are like maps." "I don't want maps," says The First Woman I've Ever Truthfully & Wholeheartedly Loved, "I want to be there…I don't need you tell me where to go." Everything about now is poetic: paper, vintage Remington, the moon. I have ideas about caressing The First Woman I've Ever Truthfully & Wholeheartedly Loved's birthmark & kissing her earlobe. This is dreamy. She's supposed to be a sap for this. I thought I could attract her reader's eye. I thought I'd be born tonight. I was & am always wrong. "You cannot be born twice," says The First Woman I've Ever Truthfully & Wholeheartedly Loved. She can tell my innermost secrets by the way I frown. She scoots down a step & asks, "What do you think about God?" Her lips look kissable. I scoot down a step, chasing her before I open my mouth. I should always chase her before opening my stupid mouth.

"I believe," I say, "God is neither man nor woman nor abstract being." The First Woman I've Ever Truthfully & Wholeheartedly Loved laughs at either my or the-God-I-describe's existence. Not blasphemously but in such a way that makes life matter. Her laughter reminds me of my cells which wish to memorize the presence of God within The First Woman I've Ever Truthfully & Wholeheartedly Loved's immaculate, rhythmic giggle.

I've been worrying about the world up until now.

We, The One Who Has My Heart—yes, she has many many names— & I, lay next to each other, atop a banig. We're at Sunset Cliffs, but the sun has already set. We hear the ocean. The wind bites our bare necks. When we shift, the banig scrapes against the dirt. The air is a thin salt. I want to hold The One Who Has My Heart so close but we're near the edge. There is a truck parked nearby. "I want to kiss you," I say. My lips are pursed but chapped & peeling. I say, "I don't like physical rejection so before you push my face away with your warm & soft & slender hands please verbally reject me." The One Who Has My Heart grabs my arm & tells me that I have her heart. *You have mine*, I want to say. I wish to crawl into her sleeve. But I'm shy. I'm shivering. I'm nervous about falling off the cliff. "If I tell you I love you," says The One Who Has My Heart, "this could mean monumental things." "You," I say, "are the monumental thing...You're not a *thing*...You're meaningful." Flashlights...the moon...the headlights of the parked truck...the slow floating of what little fog there is. "What," I ask, "do you need to know?" The One Who Has My Heart wishes not to talk: She's the One. She shuts me up because I talk too much. She can wait. She wants to be hugged. By the ground. & by me. So, we, the ground

& I, embrace her, The One Who Has My Heart. My lips are too far from the mole below her belly button. Because of the wind, my eyes are extremely dry, the driest they've ever been.

Tonight, the Organ Pavilion is empty save for some skateboarders & the occasional park dweller. We, The Love I Long For & I, sit. Again. We're always sitting & wondering & wondering. The benches are a painted metal—the car keys hanging from my pocket are scratching & tapping, making my teeth ache. We forgot forks so we can't eat our food. It doesn't matter because we're no longer hungry. So we talk & talk & talk. "What," I ask, "do you need to know?" The Love I Long For says, "How am I different?" She wears a hoodie with furry lining. She hides her lips & widens her eyes. "You," I say, "make me fly." "&," she asks, "the Others?" The Love I Long For reminds me of my past. The Others refer to *insignificance* now. The Others…What Others? "I'm freed," I assure her, "when I'm with you." I don't touch her. The Love I Long For grabs my wrists & tells me to stop being so excited. "I," she says, "can't be your cliché." She's not. If only she knew that nothing else matters. That I've never flown before. If only she knew how she could floor & sky me with a simple stare. But she wants to know. She does. She wants to know she has won my heart. She wants to know it is her, not some idea in my head. That it's she who deserves several names. She caresses my arm & I stop thinking. Planes fly & don't soar overhead. I want to scream louder than the planes. This is real. I don't know what to say for myself. Again, The Love I Long For leaves me speechless. I don't want to say anything for myself. This is for her. It's all about her. She puts her hair in a ponytail & crosses her legs. I have many *regrets* & The Love I Long For knows of them:

There's nothing wrong with my heart.

It's impossible for me to write the perfect love letter.

(I make excuses.)

"You must," says Loveliest, "make me feel different." Loveliest puts on her headphones. She sleeps in the passenger seat of my Civic. I hate the driver's seat. The lumbar support is failing & the defrosters malfunction. The windshield is filthy with dead insect legs. "You," she says, "better make me feel different." "How?" I ask. Sometimes, Loveliest asks me to be superhuman. I wish to tell her that I will spend my life trying to be superhuman but I will never come close to making her feel like what she already is: A gift. The Gift. Not a cliché. She deserves new verbs. She beauties the sky. She skies my entirety. Save the bitter love story for the ironic brokenhearted postmodernist. This is about happiness. Happiness is with Loveliest! "My emotional needs," she says, "are not being met." She is crying her eyes out. During this lifetime alone, Loveliest has had several pairs of eyes.

Today, there is everything wrong with me. The magic dies. I'm the failed romantic. I'm now the un-requiter of an unrequited love. Loveliest is the Realest. We are both tired so we fall asleep. Next to each other. Not touching.

The Realest is The Truth. The Truth lives in the previously mentioned tract house. The tract house has a cute kitchen with white-tiled countertops & a pearly white sink, the future home to stacks of unwashed dishes. We're in the front room, on the only piece of furniture in the house, a faded black secondhand futon-couch. The metal frame screeches & squeaks. The Truth & I are embracing. "I'm happy," The Truth says. & though she says she's also sad from time to time, she continues to sky my entirety. She doesn't know this, but The Truth is my first. The Truth is My First. The Truth is the first to say, "You don't scare me." Until The Truth came along, I used to believe that I could hate myself as long as someone else loved me. Until The Truth came along, it was as if I would settle for anyone who paid the slightest bit of attention to me. The Truth refuses to call my history *regrets*. The Truth is so kind. "You," I say to The Truth for some stupid self-sabotaging reason, "are selfish." Then I kiss the back of The Truth's neck. I sabotage nice things. "Take it back," says The Truth, "Prove that you don't believe that about me." I tell the Truth I can't see her right now. I rest my eyes in my palms & tears drip down my wrists. I can't breathe. I cry & cry. I gasp for air to get The Truth's attention. I take it back. I take it all back. I want to take everything back until I vanish. Here I go again: selfish. "Apparently," she says, "you have the remarkable God-given talent to tell people how they feel." The Truth's voice is so biting, but loving, really really loving. But biting. The Truth knows: I stage the world & all of its performers. I've convinced myself: The motivation of every single woman, except my mother, of course, is to break my heart. Every single woman takes everything out on me. I've been lied to, betrayed, & kicked to the other side of the world. Romance, I've come to believe, is a façade. But, if I'm always in my head, in such fiction, how can I ever connect with anyone? My heart has never really been broken. I've been an intellectual. I've convinced myself that I knew *love*. I assume The Truth feels a certain way. So, I act. I don't connect with the Real nor does she get the real me. I fuck-up often. The Truth knows. She sits against the wall next to me, her knees up, her arms folded beneath her thighs. With her head down, she looks up at me. The Truth is perfect brown, the kind the earth wants her to be. "I'm waiting," says The Truth, tapping her nose, "You can't tell me how I feel…You just can't." "I know," I say. "I'm pathetic…You should leave me." "Stop," she says, "You can't make this about you." I want to curl up into a tin can. I want to be a small lonely sardine & curl up into a tin can. I want The Truth to peel the tin back with a tiny tin key. But then the Truth would be searching for *me*. O, how fucking selfish I've always been! I've worried about her forever.

Let it be known to the world: All that matters is that The Truth, The Realest, Loveliest, The Person I Love Most, The Love I Long For, The First Woman I've Ever Truthfully & Wholeheartedly Loved, The One Who Has My Heart, loves me *without* condition. Without obsessive over-analysis. She has the most precise emotional memory. She hurts. She rejoices. Her joints ache. She listens. She hurts again. She waits for visions. She knows the pain. Of intimacy: stone, vein, ephemeral. Her teeth & jaw are important.

The Truth spreads out thin white bed sheets on the floor. We near each other. I slowly rock back & forth & back for a few minutes before I notice myself. I cup The Truth's face with the lotus of my hands. I blink. We kiss & kiss & kiss & kiss until we believe we disappear. The television crackles a little. The Truth & I have forgotten how to talk so we kiss & kiss & kiss & kiss until God becomes a little jealous. The Truth's lips, I'll say it again, are made of such good, such earthly material.

Learning to Suppose

for the grandchildren of Fortunata A. Perez

Suppose Nanay Feling pours warm Michelob
into a free McDonald's Garfield glass
& lets it chill in the refrigerator.

Suppose Nanay Feling wakes up earlier & earlier,
turns on the stove, & fries canned corned beef
& then adds eggs & more salt & more pepper.

Suppose Nanay Feling drinks the chilled Michelob,
eats the corned beef & eggs with day-old rice, then
steps outside to smoke her cigarette backwards.

Suppose Nanay Feling changes from one thinning duster
into another thinning duster, puts on her *tennis* shoes
& anxiously waits to go to Las Vegas or a local casino.

Suppose Nanay Feling is watching *The Price is Right*,
Supermarket Sweep, *Jeopardy*, & *Wheel of Fortune*,
& for some reason, a lot of boxing.

Suppose Nanay Feling is relighting the candle
for Lolo Paniong—the pancit on the altar
hardened, the bibingka now cold & full of ants.

Suppose that despite the Alzheimer's, Nanay Feling never really
forgot anything, never sat there jittery, never irritated
our parents, never asked the same questions over & over.

Suppose Nanay Feling is here right now, in her tiny bedroom—
the scotch-taped palm fronds from that long ago Palm Sunday
still rustling, empty Michelob cans on her dresser.

Suppose Nanay Feling is calling for us & saying, "Suppose
you will gonna walk to 7-Eleven & buy me
a chocolate & a Halls candy & crossword puzzle."

Suppose Nanay Feling pours us, & herself again, warm
Michelob into washed & reused flimsy Styrofoam cups
& when we all raise our cups to toast we realize that
Nanay Feling is grinning because she has already finished hers.

That One October Sixth

for Elaine Joy de la Cruz (1978-2003)

Let us rent a Winnebago *for real* this time around. There'll be no need for you to drive across these lands alone. We won't pass through/on the I-80 this time around. We will pull over & camp & sleep & keep our mouths shut. Remember that humid summer, the summer just before, in Argyle, in Chicago, & there were so many gnats trapped in our hair, on our collars, in our eyes, in our wind, in our wind? If only fireflies could escape our wind/our mouths this time. This time. Around.

Dear Joy,

I know: the epistolary form
is hella tired & uninventive.

Dear Joy,

I shall proceed anyway.

Dear Joy,

Failed Poem for You #1: Title: "When My Sister Flew Away." Useful Imagery: The tongues of serpents used to skin drums. Also, the humming. In my head. Humming. Humming. Humming.

Dear Joy,

Were you going to tell me
that you planned on wearing
the earth today?

Dear Joy,

Another fragment: Something
about you being glorious &
gorgeous.

But glorious you
need not be, you say.

I think that's what you say.

Is that you, Friend?

October 6, 2003. San Marcos, California. Friend, you are fabulous. I don't like voicemail messages. In fact, I've come to hate/fear them because of this. I'm about to drive home from work. Three. New. Messages: Noel, vague, call back. Vanessa says she just heard about you. Um. Edwina says to call back: Fuck: Fuck: Is it/this my worst nightmare?

"It's Joy, Sweetie," says Edwina, choked up. "She had an accident…She didn't make it."

Dear Joy,

That evening, that moment, that forever, that exact never, my laughter melts my lungs. I don't even know how I get here. But here, right here, is where everyone is.

I'm trying here, Friend:
Wings, grace, cliché,
cliché, esoteric letter,
cliché, cliché, angel,
so so cliché.

Here is my copout:
You are the Poem.

Profound, I know.

I know:

Lazy.

March 26, 2004

Dear Joy,

Escondido, California. Deer Park Monastery. The first ever mindfulness retreat for people of color led by Thich Nhat Hanh. Dianne. Denise. Rafa. Dabu. Jesse. Jesson. Jon S. May. All here. Bread & milk, the cosmos, never tasted so good. Eating an orange mindfully is like eating an orange while high without necessarily having smoked herb. Dabu & the others are trying to meet each other in their dreams. They like traveling, too, Friend.

Profound: You are the poem. & no. (*I never saw the flower tucked behind your ear. That was never us kneeling in front of you. I never smelled, nor continue to smell, the candles & carnations. That was not Loralei & me hesitant to walk up to say, Goodbye, before they closed the casket. Nope. The dim lighting never made me nauseous either. Nope. Never.*)

I dream of you.
On an escalator.
Hitchhiking on the side
of the road. On a Berkeley
street corner. Somewhere along
the endless I-5.
The Grapevine.
The moon ·
is a velvet skull.
& nighttime
is seaweed & Manila smoke.

Dear Joy,

I've moved to Oakland.
I'm starting grad school
today. I'm studying writing
like I'd promised.

We're gonna open
that writing center
one day.

I miss San Diego.
& you, of course.

Dear Joy,

Today, in grad school, I
learned that it is literarily
brilliant sometimes to do
this:

Dear Joy
Dear Joy Dear
Joy Dear Joy Dear

August 6, 2004

Dear Joy,

Happy Birthday! I walked around Lake Merritt this morning. I thought
that if I walked & walked & thought about every step as mindfully &
undistractedly as possible, there'd be a slight but magical chance that
you'd appear & would be walking next to me. But now you are forever
driving. To New York. Traveling to the inside of our longing. To—
Weren't the Styrofoam cups & potato chip bags & the bottle caps on
the lakeshore exactly stunning?

This afternoon is cold & depressing & grad school is a dark, intellectual & isolated place. In other words, grad school is cold & yes: depressing.

I'm on Valencia Street in the Mission. Modern Times Bookstore. There's a book, *Youthscapes: The Popular, The National, The Global*, its foreword written by George Lipsitz.

The first words:

Joy de la Cruz...

What a gift you are, Friend.

May 26, 2005

Dear Joy,   *(Dear Joy,*

There's an internship   *I haven't written a sad*
named after you!   *poem in ages.)*

Is it because I never cried at the funeral?

Sometimes, these days, I *do* cry in the morning, & my ribcages open, & my throat is warm, coated with ink, blood & what I wish to believe is you, Friend.

Dear Joy,

Everyone travels to the Bay
every October. Once in August,
for your birthday, Friend.

Dear Joy,

I'm writing a novel about
my mother!

I promise it'll be better than that
silly syntactically offensive
poem I used to perform
over & over.

(*Thank you for loving that silly
poem.*)

(*You & my mother look alike
in my guided meditations—
you & she have the same
silhouette.*)

By the way, your baby sister & your mama came to my show in SoMa last night. Your mama made your sister who then made your mama give me two $20 bills to support my/our hungry artist dreams.

April 29, 2006

Dear Joy,

LA Uprising: 14 years ago!
I'm graduating today.

(& I don't visit your
headstone.)

Dear Joy,

Every *sixth* is Joy Day.

Dear Joy,

Dianne named a character
Hope to honor &
remember you in her play
the year after.

Dear Joy,

We have a Black president!

& *hope* is part of the
popular imagination.

Dear Joy,

Stuff you most likely know: Christine is a high school teacher in Vallejo. Rene is a high school teacher in LA, a comedian on his off-hours. Dianne creates parols out of bottle caps & manages programs for an arts nonprofit in the Bay. Steve went to film school & he's married now! Arash: still a hustler, the safe kind, did you see him on *How I Met Your Mother*? & Vejea is Professor Jennings.

Remember when we were naming ourselves & we cleverly thought of *Freedom Writers* & we discovered the story of those high school students. Well, there's a fucking movie based on them! &. &. It's mad problematic. Hella problematic. (*Although, I can't stop watching it.*) Hilary Swank, do-gooder white lady teacher, ends racial conflict between Black, Latino & Cambodian youth in Long Beach. That ain't freedom, I agree. It's neoliberalism. & colonialism. We're totally more deserving of the name.

Dear Joy,

Let us rent a Winnebago
this time around.
This time around.
This time around.
Yes.
This time around.
We will not
pass on/through the I-80.
We will turn around &
head back to San Diego,
here, where everyone
seems to be right now.

(*In my head.*)

(*In my waiting. & Waiting.*)

Dear Joy,

You
keep
wearing
this earth
without
letting us
know!

Dear Joy,

Why didn't you tell me you were going to wear the *sky* tonight? I feel so terribly underdressed.

Prologue to a Novel about How to Achieve Healthier-Looking Skin

First, my primary care physician...then the allergist...& now the dermatologist, with way too much confidence, has misdiagnosed me. Regardless of what they all say, I'm convinced that this isn't eczema. These, the scars & rough patches on my forehead & all over, may very well be what my father has suggested all along: The marks of a prolonged & haunting colonization.

"Your skin," says my father, "is reacting to centuries of subjection, or subjugation, or something like that one."

"Anak," adds my mother, "your skin is not beautiful. You should go home in Philippines because those humidity there, you know that one, is good for the complexion—it makes superstar."

I collect flakes of dry & dead skin underneath my fingernails. My neck is raw & pink. My girlfriend doesn't mind the raw & pink of my neck, the maps. My girlfriend thinks it's cute how I can't control my scratching. It's all about the passion. If I scratched with vigor & intention, could I disappear?

Colonization & eczema have always been the issue. Most of the time, it's hard to believe my father, the same man who a few months ago blamed my skin condition on my tendency to believe in God. I wonder why God wouldn't have rather made my skin like a paper bag, wet, crumpled, predictable. Why not coffee brown? Or apocalyptic brown? Why pink? Why raw? Why maps?

My grandmother often tells me I'm special. "YOU," she says, "ARE SUPERHERO." People don't understand.

(*My grandmother will die during the course of this novel & I won't feel special anymore.*)

At this point, you might be thinking: Why is it always ethnic *identity politics* & the supposed sanctity of the close-knit nuclear & extended family with these *underrepresented marginalized minority multicultural* writers? Perhaps you also are confused by the ways in which *multicultural* signifies everything but white. Why must you exploit your *Otherness* in order to gain sympathy? You might also assume that this novel will be an imaginative *discourse* on the *diaspora* of my people. You might consider *discourse* & *diaspora* to be keywords saved for academic writing because, depending on your *positionality* as a reader, my casual use of such a word like *diaspora* preceding the phrase *of my people* may make you feel uncomfortable, guilty, stuck, left-out even, like the kid picked last on the kickball field. (Trust me, I will always be the last one picked.) & if you consider yourself not left-out, & you are, in fact, *my people*, you're a little ashamed that I perform my "intelligence" & carelessly slip into scholarly modalities. This writing, you might say, is so overdetermined. Too academic, you add. Are you writing for educated white readers? On with the fucking story, School Boy! Two answers to your thinking: 1) *This novel was never intended for you but for my grandmothers, the one who will die in this novel, & the other who has been dead for a long time & was illiterate when she was alive &* 2) *I am strangeness.* I am strangeness not because I feel & thus am hyper-marginalized. Or that I feel & thus believe I am illegal. But because if you were to trace the pink patches on my forehead, behind my ears, hovering about my hairline, across my neck, down the center of my back, along my spine, across my arms, you'd notice the makings & markings of an archipelago, & *that, that* constitutes strangeness, perhaps an ugliness you've learned to ignore.

My girlfriend refuses the colonization thesis. In her decolonial imaginary, my girlfriend predicts that the archipelago will form as a fragmented mass first on my back, then toward my hips & ribs, up & down my chest, all over my legs, & behind my knees. Eventually, there will be no need for me to get a tribal tattoo to feel closer to my indigenous roots. Eventually, I will become those very roots. Laugh all you want at my scars, I say. Call them hickeys. Tell the world it's cancerous, it's contagious—*His wounds throb & throb!* Curse me. Remind me that I'm nothing special. But one day, one extraordinary day, when the sunlight no longer makes my scars glow, when perspiration no longer makes me violently claw at my eyebrows, legs & neck, when I stop scratching & learn how to sleep through the night again, I will have become my dreams, & everyone will do everything in their power to live their modest & marginal lives *on* what will become of *me*. On *my* skin.

I shall be mud. I promise.

I cough up thick phlegm & spit into tiny wads of toilet paper: my asthma is getting worse. There's no clear explanation for this one. It may have something to do with me not being able to breathe on land. But then again, when I was six, when I was tossed into the swimming pool to learn how to swim, I nearly drowned, which proves that despite what American soldiers believed, I am no amphibian. I'd simply like to know why I'm doomed to change.

"Change is good," assures my father. "Change means the death of power."

112

My girlfriend applies hydrocortisone cream 2.5% & triamcinolone cream 0.1% to my wounds. When my condition is at its worst, my girlfriend applies the good stuff: floucinonide ointment 0.05% & elidel cream 1%, the latter of which is safe for the face & for the delicate skin of infants but has also for some reason been known to cause lymphoma in lab rats. My girlfriend smells of an elegy. I kiss her nose. In this novel, she thinks I'll be proposing to her. (I'm not ready.) I just want to sleep beside her. I just want to hold her hand long enough so that I no longer think about scratching...*I've got it!* I shall launch a mass movement for all of our peoples to return to the Philippines. We will all go back to where we came from. For the sake of our skin.

"But you," says my girlfriend, "are metamorphosing into the land of which you've forever dreamt." Indeed, I am pink & toxic. & my girlfriend is correct: I have no reason to leave myself. My late uncle, one of my father's older brothers, would be of a different solution. My uncle used to say that for the Philippines to make progress in this world order we'd have to kill the entire population & start anew.

"They," my uncle would say, "are all backwards."

"That," I'd respond, "is not true. Plus, that, my dear uncle, constitutes *genocide*."

Wouldn't it be easier if *I* just killed *myself?*

But come to think of it, if I did, in fact, go ahead & kill myself, where, oh, where would all the people live?

Notes

The epigraph & crux of the book title are from José Garcia Villa, *Doveglion: Collected Poems*, ed. John Edwin Cowen (New York: Penguin, 2008), 47.

"Violent Hero" samples from Grandmaster Flash & the Furious Five, "The Message" (Sugar Hill Records, 1982), & from Eazy-E's verse in West Coast Rap All-Stars, "We're All in the Same Gang" (Warner Bros. Records, 1990).

"Crayoning the King: On Discipline" draws from various sources—references to *discipline* are from Michel Foucault, *Discipline & Punish: The Birth of the Prison*, trans. Alan Sheridan (New York: Vintage Books, 1977, 1995), 152-153; references to Carlos Argentino Daneri are from Jorge Luis Borges, "The Aleph," in *The Aleph and Other Stories*, trans. Andrew Hurley (New York: Viking Penguin, 1998), 118-133; there's a nod to Kiese Laymon's title essay & book "How to Slowly Kill Yourself and Others in America," in *How to Slowly Kill Yourself and Others in America* (Chicago: Agate Bolden, 2013); a quick reference is made to Dead Prez's song "Discipline" (Columbia Records, 2000); references here to *interdisciplinarity* are from Trinh T. Minh-ha, *Framer Framed: Film Scripts and Interviews* (New York: Routledge, 1992), 165.

"You, Praxes for Loving" samples & reconfigures lines from various poems: Mila D. Aguilar, "A Comrade is as Precious as a Rice Seedling" & "The Peoples' Poem," in *A Comrade is as Precious as a Rice Seedling* (New York: Kitchen Table Press, 1985), 38, 11; Chrystos, "I Walk in the History of My People," in *This Bridge Called My Back: Writings by Radical Women of Color*, ed. Gloria Anzaldúa & Cherríe Moraga (New York: Kitchen Table/Women of Color Press, 1984), 60; Audre Lorde, "Women on

Trains," in *The Marvelous Arithmetics of Distance: Poems 1987-1992* (New York: W.W. Norton & Company, 1994), 31-33; Audre Lorde, "Stations," in *Collected Poems of Audre Lorde* (W.W. Norton & Company, 2000), 367-368.

"The Girl Who Fills Her E's" samples a line from Mila D. Aguilar, "A Comrade is as Precious as a Rice Seedling," in *A Comrade is as Precious as a Rice Seedling* (New York: Kitchen Table Press, 1985), 38, & quickly borrows & nods to the notion of *biomythography* in Audre Lorde, *Zami: A New Spelling of My Name* (Berkeley: Crossing Press, 1982).

"For Your Solitudes Crowded with Loneliness: Letter to My Nephew" borrows part of its title from Bob Kaufman, *Solitudes Crowded with Loneliness* (New York: New Directions, 1965). This work also directly quotes the character Buzz Lightyear in *Toy Story*, performed by Tim Allen (1995; Burbank, CA: Walt Disney Home Video, 1996), DVD.

"But Life Goes On" samples lyrics from two songs by Tupac Shakur: "Starin' Thru My Review" (Death Row Records, 1997) & "Life Goes On" (Death Row Records, 1996).

"Stranger Here: Oral History (*U.S. v. Narciso & Perez*)" is an oral history that includes text that has been sampled, cut & rearranged from interviews that the author conducted with his mother, Leonora M. Perez, during the month of March 2010.

"*Leonora, archive of:* Film Transcripts" contains the transcripts from the film/video series titled *Leonora, archive of* (2013), an experiment in oral history, performance & documentary filmmaking by the author.

"Phenomenology of Superhero" is a response to the *Superhero Portrait Invitational* (2015), & was performed for a collaborative event hosted by

Art Span & Quiet Lightning Reading Series at the Modern Eden Gallery in the North Beach neighborhood of San Francisco, CA. Explicit references are made to the following artworks: Helice Wen's *Atomu (Astro Boy)*; Brianna Angelakis's *The Storm Begins*; Scott Holloway's *Aquaman*; Daniel J. Valadez's *Wolverine*; Primary Hughes's *Daughter of Themyscira (Wonder Woman)*; Monty Guy's *Rogue*; Adam Caldwell's *Cyclops*; Bradley Platz's *Odin's Son (Thor)*; Rich Pelligrino's *A Dinner Party (Catwoman)*; & Henry Shreiber's *What a Mouse! (Mighty Mouse)*. The exhibition can be viewed at: *http://www.moderneden.com/collections/superhero*. Additionally, this essay samples Ice-T, "Colors," in *Colors: Soundtrack* (Warner Bros. Records, 1988). & lastly, this essay directly quotes from Sara Ahmed, *Queer Phenomenology: Orientations, Objects, Others* (Durham: Duke University Press, 2006), 38, 175, 168, respectively.

"That One October Sixth" is dedicated to the late & fabulous Elaine Joy de la Cruz (1978-2003). To be clear, it was written to honor Joy in 2008 & thus so much has changed since then. The original sentiment/narrative remains. Historian George Lipsitz writes: "Joy de la Cruz died in a car crash on a Nevada highway on October 6, 2003. She was only twenty-five years old. A much-admired spoken-word performer and feminist activist, her brilliant potential will now never be realized fully. She grew up as the first truly transnational generation of youth, an immigrant daughter whose first language was Tagalog. For those of us who knew her in San Diego where she went to college or in the San Francisco Bay Area where she was raised, Joy was our 'morning star'—a planet that burns so brightly in the eastern sky that everyone who sees it knows a new dawn is coming." SEE George Lipsitz, "Foreword: Midnight's Children: Youth Culture in the Age of Globalization," in *Youthscapes: The Popular, the National, the Global*, ed. Sunaina Maira & Elizabeth Soep (Philadelphia: University of Pennsylvania Press, 2005), xii.

Acknowledgments

Earlier versions of some of these poems, essays, stories & fragments, some under different titles, previously appeared in or were performed during the following: "Violent Hero" & "Cough Drop: An Artifact" were first performed at LitCrawl SF for the panel *Six Authors/Six Genres* (2015), the latter then appeared in *TAYO Literary Magazine* (2016); "Crayoning the King: On Discipline" appeared on *TAYO Literary Magazine*'s Blog (2014-2015); "You, Praxes for Loving" appeared in *The Feminist Wire* (2015); "The Girl Who Fills Her E's" appeared in *TAYO Literary Magazine* (2016) & in *vitriol* (2017); "For Your Solitudes Crowded with Loneliness: Letter to My Nephew" was first performed at the symposium *From Trauma to Catharsis: Performing the Asian Avant-Garde* hosted by the California Institute for Integral Studies (2014), & later appeared in *Eleven Eleven* (2015); "But Life Goes On" appeared on the author's website (2013); "Stranger Here: Oral History (*U.S. v. Narciso & Perez*)" is a monologue from *You Will Gonna Go Crazy* (2011), a multimedia performance work first commissioned by Kularts, Inc., San Francisco, & is forthcoming under a different title in the edited volume *CALIFORNIA DREAMING: Movement & Place in the Asian American Imaginary*, eds. Lucy Mae San Pablo Burns & Christine Bacareza Balance (University of Hawai'i Press, Forthcoming); "Phenomenology of Superhero" was first performed for Quiet Lightning Reading Series & ArtSpan in response to the *Superhero Portrait Invitational* (2015) at the Modern Eden Gallery in San Francisco, CA; "What Saddens Sardines: A Romantic Outcry" & "Learning to Suppose" both appeared in *TAYO Literary Magazine* (2016); "That One October Sixth" appeared in the anthology *Nexus: Complicating Community and Centering the Self: A 20 Year Retrospective of a College-Based Community Center*, eds. Edwina Welch et al. (Cognella, 2015); "Prologue to a Novel about How to Achieve Healthier-Looking Skin" appeared in *vitriol* (2017); & finally, the following works were collected in a chapbook titled *Phenomenology of Superhero* (Red Bird Chapbooks, 2016): "Crayoning the King: On Discipline"; "Violent Hero"; "Prologue to Novel about How to Achieve Healthier-Looking Skin"; "For Your Solitudes Crowded with Loneliness: Letter to My Nephew"; & "Phenomenology of Superhero."

I'd like to express my deepest, most humblest, most infinite gratitude to *you*, to *you* who have held me down in your special magical ways, to *all of you* who already know what it is: the love of my life, my kasama in the struggle; my parents; my brothers & sisters-in-law; my beautiful & intelligent nieces & nephews; my dear cousins; my aunties & uncles; my lolas & lolos; my dearest homies from San Diego to Los Angeles to the Bay & all over; mga kasama ko/mis compas; my writing peers; my colleagues, past & present; all of my mentors, past & present; & all of my students, past & present. I'd like to especially thank the following individuals for their generous reading of & feedback for this manuscript in its various stages: Jai Arun Ravine; Eunsong Kim; Kimberly Alidio; Denizen Kane; & Vejea Jennings. Maraming salamat to Amy Abito for capturing the vision of the book in the cover design. & lastly, muchas mad gracias to Lori Jareo & Kevin Walzer of WordTech Editions who've helped this first book find a home & materialize.

About the Author

Jason Magabo Perez writes, performs & teaches. Perez is the author of *Phenomenology of Superhero* (Red Bird Chapbooks, 2016). Perez's writing has appeared in *Witness, TAYO, vitriol, Eleven Eleven, Mission at Tenth,* & *The Feminist Wire.* Perez has written, developed & performed two live multimedia performance-theatre works: *The Passion of El Hulk Hogancito* (2009) & *You Will Gonna Go Crazy* (2011), the latter of which was commissioned by Kularts, Inc. & funded by a Challenge America Grant from the National Endowment for the Arts. Perez has performed at notable venues such as the National Asian American Theater Festival, International Conference of the Philippines, Yerba Buena Center for the Arts, Asian Art Museum, & La Jolla Playhouse. An alumnus of the VONA Writing Workshops for Writers of Color, Perez holds an M.F.A. in Writing & Consciousness from New College of California & a dual Ph.D. in Communication & Ethnic Studies from University of California, San Diego. Currently, Perez is an Assistant Professor of English at California State University, San Bernardino.

www.jasonmagaboperez.com